Requiem for Greed

Cast of Characters (in order of appearance):

Adam Smith –A Scottish social philosopher and a pioneer of political economy. One of the key figures of the Scottish Enlightenment, Smith is the author of *The Theory of Moral Sentiments* as well as *An Inquiry into the Nature and Causes of the Wealth of Nations*. The latter, usually abbreviated as *The Wealth of Nations*, is considered his magnum opus and the first modern work of economic theory. Smith is widely cited as the father of modern economics and Capitalism.

Karl Marx - A German philosopher, sociologist, economic historian, journalist, and revolutionary socialist who developed the socio-political theory of Marxism. His ideas have since played a significant role in the development of social science and the socialist political movement. He published various books during his lifetime, with the most notable being *The Communist Manifesto* (1848) and *Das Kapital* (1867–1894).

Politician

Older Man - Financial News Co-Anchor

Younger Man - Financial News Co-Anchor

Younger Woman - Financial News Co-Anchor

MBA #1 – Male

MBA #2 – Female

MBA #3 – Male

Central Banker

Professor - MBA Program

Banker #1

Banker #2

Banker #3

Banker #4

Location: USA

Time: 2001-2009

1

History of Crisis

Prologue: Adam Smith and Karl Marx

Adam Smith

Having written "The Wealth of Nations,"

I look sadly at my creation

Our great society's degradation

Causes nothing, - but trepidation.

Where did I go wrong?

All I wanted was free trade all day long

Where competition and hard work got along

To make the economy strong.

The invisible hand rules all

and self-interest makes it whole,

but the builder of the proverbial wall

is as important as St. Paul.

Yes, I see that I've created greed

Dollar bill is the newest creed

This society's illness, indeed

Is spreading fast I must, sadly, concede.

Karl Marx

Dialectic materialism, labor struggle, and fetishism

Don't tell me I did not warn.

I told you in Das Kapital this would be a war!

A war between the classes,

You don't need to wear glasses

To see there is much unrest in the masses!

Accumulation and wealth creation

Are nothing more than aberration

The proletariat has nothing to lose

but its chains!

The specter haunts…

(clicks his fingers) and the bourgeoisie wanes…

Adam Smith

Pardon me! Whatever happened to the Eastern Block?

Tell me what happened to the worldwide revolution?

Your teaching was just a crock!

You were the problem, not the solution!

Karl Marx

If I was the problem, so were you

You need not look far to see what transpired

A couple of busts – and the middle class said "adieu"

And real estate values simply expired!

Adam Smith and Karl Marx

What happened here and whose teachings are right?

Who is the culprit that started this mess?

Who gave this situation a green light?

And put the economy in distress?

ACT 1

Scene 1 - Politician Speaking in Front of Audience

Politician

My predecessor many years ago

Promised a chicken in every pot

How about a house? You don't need "dough"

Let me see what you've got!

Are you unemployed? So, what's the problem?

You have no credit? Hey, so what?

You have no money?

Here is your answer:

Just don't forget to vote!

Everyone has to own a house

Isn't this the American Dream?

Whether you are from Poland or from Laos

Borrow to the extreme!

I'll talk to Fannie

I'll talk to Freddie

They better take good notes!

Get those moving trucks all ready

And don't forget to vote!

No one needs those lending guidelines

When election is at stake!

And when my name is in the headlines...

You will eat chicken; and I'll have steak!

Scene 2 - Financial Network Program

Older Man - Financial News Co-Anchor

Whether the market moves up

Younger Man - Financial News Co-Anchor

Or if it goes down

Younger Woman - Financial News Co-Anchor

Or if it goes sideways

Younger Man - Financial News Co-Anchor

Or if it stands still

Older Man - Financial News Co-Anchor

We are here to tell you

What to do with your money:

If you have any money,

Then go in for the kill!

Pull out our crystal balls *(everyone pulls out a crystal ball)*

Look at the stars formation *(starry sky)*

We will predict inflation

Yes, we are on a roll!

Younger Man - Financial News Co-Anchor

Eat your heart out, Nostradamus

How was your rate of return?

Yours was not much of a promise

How much did YOUR Prophesies earn?

Younger Woman - Financial News Co-Anchor

Finance is the new religion

And we are its highest priests

We lead the investors' legions

Into financial bliss...

Scene 3 - Three MBA Candidates at a Bar

MBA #1 – Male

I grew up in Ohio, my father was an engineer

He has been using retorts and other scientific gear

He took me to his lab several times a year

When I was growing up, there was nothing I wanted more

Than to become a "science pioneer"

I wanted to invent, I wanted to produce

I loved the smell of the factory

I loved the smell of the factory

I loved the smell of the factory

Please pass me my Grey Goose

And everyone knew each other

And everyone said "good day"

And the workers would always gather

At a tavern to watch the game.

It seemed like this would last forever

But, alas, nothing ever does

We heard the news one morning

And the whole town was abuzz

At the factory, at a meeting

A few guys in *Brooks Brothers* suits

Announced that they were completing

A divestiture...

Pass the "Absolut"

We were told we're not efficient,

Human labor costs way too high,

Our product line will move to China,

Here's two-week's severance, now "good-bye."

Yes, my choices became crystal clear,

I could stay and collect welfare checks,

Or become like those guys in full gear

Flashing *Brook Brothers* suits and a ROLEX.

If you cannot beat them, join them

Bury childhood ambitions, old guy.

Only once in a while I dream of my father,

And his retorts... and I want to cry.

MBA #2 – Female

When I was a little girl

I read one book after another

I read before school, I read in classes

I read "Gone with the Wind" to my little brother

My dream was to teach;

The souls of young ones

I wanted to reach.

But my class mates were so cruel,

They would make fun of me,

It was so dreadful for me in school,

That I hated them to the *n-th* degree,

But the best revenge I could think of,

Was to become so very rich,

I gave up Dostoyevsky and Goethe,

To become a corporate bitch!

I was always an average student

Having no particular skills

So my uncle suggested that it would be prudent

that I pick up a trade to pay the bills

He suggested the plumbing profession-

'In demand and you make a few bucks'

but I'd like to produce a confession,

it requires some work, it is for schmucks!

My mom's grandpa was a well-known baker-

I would drive a delivery truck

But, good grief, to become a bread maker???

Waking up before dawn is for schmucks!

And my father, a junior pastor

Every Sunday he gathers his flock,

He prepares a sermon, and talks to his Master

But the money he makes is for schmucks

No plumbing or baking professions.

My ambitions are greater than that

Surely, God will forgive my transgressions

I will enter this race as a rat!

ALL THREE MBAs

We forgot our childhood ambitions

When we entered the kingdom of greed

You are plebs; we are your patricians

Money rules, money rules, yes, indeed!!

Scene 4 – Central Banker Testifies Before Congress

Central Banker

The empirical literature holds the view

Our economic policy is brand new

It is the New Economy, the New Economy

Give the bankers complete autonomy, COMPLETE AUTONOMY!

Our economic policy is a factor of astronomy!

Look at the stars! They move in perfect chaos

They don't collide, so what's the big fuss?

Banks are the forefront of the financial intermediation

And the market's overall sophistication

Will indefinitely postpone the stagnation

We are on course to become the greatest nation!

Due to increased product mutation

We will achieve risk mitigation

Yes, the degree of sophistication

Will surely provide a complete relaxation

And Independence from regulations!

We want flexibility that yields stability

From which investors will feel tranquility

And, even, God willing, profitability!

This is a trend that Mao would loath

This lead to an unprecedented growth!

Growth of houses, growth of cars

Growth of boats and Growth of bars

Greatness is good, and there is no harm

Don't get a fixed loan, do get an ARM!

Greater expenditures cause job creation!

We will become an insatiable nation!

Scene 5 – Financial Network

Older Man - Financial News Co-Anchor

The Dow is at 10,000

And soon it will go higher

Never mind the old bear market

It will soon retire

The S&P Index will move even higher

We are so bullish

WE ARE SO BULLISH-

The bear is on the pyre!

Younger Man - Financial News Co-Anchor

Our panel of experts is bullish on stocks

They love home builders, George Bush, and Iraq

They love Lehman Brothers, Bear Stearns, Goldman Sachs

They go bananas for steel, beer, and drugs!

ALL OF THEM

Hooray for the bull market! Hooray for the bull market!

Hooray for the bull market!

Bear market is for schmucks!

Scene 6 - MBA Program – In class

Professor - MBA Program

Three hundred and seventy years ago

If you lived in Amsterdam

And sold tulip bulbs

That was some racket!

I am telling you, bro'

You could buy a brothel near the Dam

Bulbs were bought and sold dozens of times

And people made money hand over fist

But as we all know, what rapidly climbs

Drops even further. Was everyone pissed!

Fast-forward to pre-Great Depression times

I want you to meet a pyramid schemer

His name was Ponzi, his trade was lies

I would not call him "the great redeemer"

Insider trading was a big gig

That sent a few "greats" to the slammer

Come on, men,

If you want to act like pigs

Don't be afraid to get hit by the hammer

Fast-forward again, and what do we see?

What is going on in the land of the free?

Selling the sizzle, not selling the steak,

Dot com buccaneers are claiming their stake

Where brand new economy is the new norm

Who says we need profits? You've been misinformed!

Your Internet presence is all that we need

Again and again, our motto is greed!

And suddenly crap-dot-com company's

Net worth is huge

But where is the product?

Oh, don't be a stooge!

We need no products nor profits we need

When we go public, your asse(t)s will bleed

And through smoke and mirrors, abuses, and dust

Our country's economy finally went bust

13

The dot com adventure brought ruin to many

Which brings us directly to Freddie and Fannie.

Bell Rings

Scene 7 – MBA Students at a Bar

MBA #1 – Male

What will I do when I am a partner?

What will I do?

I will buy a sleek car and a boat,

Drink Dom Perignon,

Buy my wife a mink coat,

I will have a secretary, no, personal assistant

I will smoke cigars, but only Monte Cristo

What will I do when I am a partner?

I will go around the world in a plane that my company charters

At my subordinates I will look down my nose

And everyone will whisper, "Look, there he goes"

I will demand respect and submission

My name will be under my company's mission

I plan to watch sports events from the skybox

And I will receive lots of company's stocks!

MBA #3 – Male

What will I do when I am on top?

What will I do when I am on top?

When I am in charge, oh, heads will be chopped!

I'll drive the revenue working non-stop

Working 'round the clock, you bet I will

My only God will be the dollar bill

Day and night, night and day

Do you feel sick? Well, take a pill!

Get with the program!

You know the drill!

I will be ruthless, my goal's crystal clear

I am on this earth to build a career!

MBA #2 – Female

When I'm in charge of a large corporation

When I'm in charge of a large corporation

No doubt, I will get a standing ovation

When I see my old class mates

Twenty years after graduation

(I am not sure this won't give them a severe constipation)

They will be green with envy over my grandiose station

I will impress the aging class queen

Who, back then, was so vain and so very mean

She wouldn't even look my way

But here I am on full display

Look at me, look what I got

My husband is young and he is so HOT!

I live in a penthouse and I own a yacht

And you my old buddies

Let's see what you've got!

Revenge is so sweet!

I am a big shot!

All MBA's Chorus

When we're on top

When we head corporations

When we become the captains of our nation

When we fly over in our corporate jets

And sit at the company's box at the Met

When we receive all our options and stocks...

Politician (Suddenly Appearing)

And don't you forget the good old ballot box!

Scene 8 – Central Banker Talking to the Public

Central Banker

Our country's growth is unprecedented

It's a historic moment that should be documented

This fact that was highly anticipated

Our country's old economy had become antiquated

Consumers unite in their determination

To make shopping and buying their second vocation

To shop 'til they drop, but with a sense of elation

Be sure that they use credit cards for cremation

Let's see what we have that is still left untapped

Let's see if we add even more to the debt

Where can we possibly get some more cash?

Extract it from equity! Don't be abashed!

Your home is your castle, but, also, is your bank

Here is your check - See? It is nice and blank!

Scene 9 - Financial Network

Older Man - Financial News Co-Anchor

The Guru has spoken, the Guru has spoken

We know that the old paradigm has been broken

We need to buy houses, cars, and consume

This trend just won't end, I would humbly assume.

But what will transpire if your credit is sub-par?

Younger Woman - Financial News Co-Anchor

No worries, he said, you're still a super star!

Your credit, your job, and your house – they won't matter

That's what I heard from the board room chatter

The rumor I heard that persists downtown

Is that housing prices will never come down.

Younger Man - Financial News Co-Anchor

Real estate values will never come down

That's what I hear in LA and Miami

That's what I hear in Chicago and Dallas

Don't be a moron – move into a palace!

ALL THREE

The Guru has spoken, the Guru has spoken!

He told us the old paradigm has been broken,

We'll wait for the bankers to make their best move

No doubt we'll see that they'll be in the groove!

Scene 10 – Bankers Attending a Meeting at a Resort

Banker #1

Ladies and Gentlemen, let me present

The opportunity that was God-sent

The currents have changed and deregulation

Will have a huge impact on our nation

Banker #2

And from your mouth right-up to God's ears

This is the best news that I've heard in years

This is a green light to make, it appears,

Lots of new loans (and profits), so CHEERS!

Banker #3

Political winds blowing into our coffer

The public demands, and we surely will offer,

Loans with terms no one understands

And then we re-sell them for Euros and yen

Banker #4

You have no income, but we'll gladly approve you

Your credit is crap, not a problem at all

Your house is half-burnt, take the money, we beg you

We make borrowing as simple as a stroll in the mall

All Bankers

We hear the message, and it's loud and clear

Give money away and collect a huge fee

Lots of new products we will engineer

No restraints, no limits – a huge lending spree!

Scene 11 - Adam Smith and Karl Marx

Karl Marx

Do you understand what is happening here?

Adam Smith

I have a feeling they are all deranged

Karl Marx

The voice of reason has simply disappeared

Adam Smith

Let's wait and see, and hope for a change.

END OF ACT 1

ACT II

Scene 1 – Central banker and Politician in the Restaurant

Central Banker

A bubble's not likely, but there is a sign of frost

The prices in some areas are not sustainable

Politician

Excuse me, Mr. Banker, but I am a bit lost

Can you confirm my re-election is attainable?

Central Banker

The whole country is infatuated with real estate

The mantra is to buy, buy, buy

But I am not sure that's so great

Politician

Then, I can kiss my political career "good bye"….

Central Banker

It seems we are the victims of our own success

I may, in fact, regret my own actions

Should I assume that this becomes a mess

I am afraid to think of a chain reaction.

Politician

This can't be happening to me, old fool

I did not get my Ph.D. in Economics

It was a miracle that I had finished school-

My education came from reading comics

My superheroes, Steel Man and Underdog

They always found ways to get out of trouble

We better find the way to clear up this fog

And not utter a word about a "bubble"!

Scene 2 – MBAs in the Business District

MBA #1 (Rapping)

I am armed with an MBA degree

I have my HP 12C and a Blackberry

I am interviewing for a job!

I will show them what I've got!

I want a management job from the start

I want a big bonus; I am not faint of heart

Let someone else work at K-Mart

I'm the best of the best; I'm a real work of art

My ego is huge, and you're not worth my fart

My salary is six figures, from the start

I know my pie charts and the Theory of Motivation

I even know how to use standard deviation

I know economics and I know NPV

My salary will be a small country's GDP

Supply and demand is my favorite subject

I'm in demand when money is no object

And my third car's marginal utility

Tops the theory of relativity

Price elasticity and market share

Will help me decide where to make my hair

I am the hero of the day

I'm a freshly-minted MBA!

Chorus of MBAs

We are the best, we know it all

After we graduate, we'll take on our role

We'll turn our country into a huge shopping mall...

Central Banker (Quietly)

Just don't be surprised to get a margin call

Scene 3 – Financial Network

Older Man - Financial News Co-Anchor

Economists tell us that we should not be worrying

The impact on the markets will be contained

Real estate values will still be soaring

This time it's different, the wise men explained

Younger Man - Financial News Co-Anchor

There is still liquidity aplenty, or so I hear

The music is playing and the chairs are set

It's hard to imagine that funds disappear

But even if so, we still shouldn't fret

Younger Woman - Financial News Co-Anchor

Our experts and guest remain somewhat bullish

They expect neither a housing bubble nor a shock

And in the hope of not seeming foolish

Get out there to make a few bucks!

ALL THREE

When the music stops, look for your chair

When the music stops, it had better be there

When the music stops, please do not despair

When the music stops....

Scene 4 – Politician and Central Banker in a Smoke-Filled Office

Politician

Can someone please explain what is happening?

Can someone please tell me what's going on?

Housing prices are beginning to plummet

Many mortgage payments are not being made

This situation is making me vomit

Everything was going so great!

We had the situation well under control

Houses were built and fortunes were made

Yes, there were excesses (or so I was told)

But now it seems more like the problems cascade

Yes, people don't save and live beyond their means

But don't tell us what we can or can't afford

That's why we had a solution for this -

We sold our debt to the rest of the world

We sold our paper and we bought their stuff

Who cares that we became money jugglers?

We've created engineers of fluff!

But having to deal with it is pretty ugly!

Central Banker

This boom is surely becoming a bust

And "toxic assets" are everywhere

The rating agencies we cannot trust

This looks like the Great Depression, I swear.

Politician

We will not panic, we will stay calm

We won't let capitalism disappear

This feels as if someone just dropped The Bomb

(Phone rings)

The bankers just called, and they are all in tears

Scene 5 – Central banker with Bankers in the Conference Room

Banker #1

Companies are closing down left and right

Nobody wants our paper anymore

Investors want their money, but the money is tight

And when we leave the building, it's through the back door

This is not what we had envisioned

The situation has gone out of control

We will be forced to make a decision

Who can we burden with scapegoat's role?

Banker #2

Our companies are downgraded

We are now as good as junk

Our old glory is all, but faded

Let's all go out and get drunk!

Banker #3

At least being drunk will add some liquidity

Not to the treasury though

We should expect the rate of morbidity

To rise, if there is no "dough"

The public demands human sacrifice

What to do? Let's discuss,

How about to throw dice to create

A sacrificial lamb among us?

ALL BANKERS

Who among us will be brought down

From the Olympus to the pyre

Who will make sure that we are around

To light the sacrificial fire?

Whoever has chosen a different path

He, who is not with us

1 out of 4, you do the math,

Will be thrown under the bus

There is no loyalty when money is at stake

There are no friends or allies

The law of the jungle rules, don't make a mistake

The weak among us, surely, dies.

Central Banker

What do you have to say in your defense?

You are a bunch of goofs

The situation is very tense

The pressure is through the roof

I have politicians breathing down my neck

Their priorities are crystal clear

If we can't find the solution for this wreck

We will get a kick in the rear

And then you can kiss your careers goodbye

Along with all your corporate perks

Your recently purchased black shoes and black tie

Will be eaten in the closet where moth lurks.

Don't cry, I am here with my arsenal

We still have the good ol' printing press

This will stay in history as bacchanal

That ended yet one more excess.

Banker #1

What do we do with number 4?

Do we bail him out or not?

Central Banker

No - he goes down, but not before

You tighten the merger knot

From this point on, listen to me

And listen well, my friends

Don't even think of taking a pee

Without my permission and without my command.

You will comply with all my demands

And won't be nay-sayers

Because at the end, your reward will be

Lots of help from our taxpayers

And the good old printing press will work overtime

And money will flow again

And the cash register's beautiful chime

Will calm down the soul and the brain

Central Banker and Fellow Bankers

This is a calamity beyond our worst fears

Our only hope is taxpayers, it appears

Oh, gods of finance, don't let us disappear

We feel it in our guts, that our demise is near,

Banker #4 (suddenly appearing)

(But a golden parachute will carry me well into my golden years)

Scene 6 – Financial Network

Older Man - Financial News Co-Anchor

It does not seem that things will end pretty

The markets are holding on by only a thread

Default is a certainty, and with some pity

I'd like to announce that the system is dead

Younger Man - Financial News Co-Anchor

Run for the exit, run for your money

Panic sets in, there is no solution

Everything was so cheerful and sunny

Will this situation have a resolution?

Our crystal balls were completely defected

Older Woman - Financial News Co-Anchor

Do you think they were assembled in China?

Younger Man - Financial News Co-Anchor

Our panel of experts was highly respected

Younger Woman - Financial News Co-Anchor

Just like the criminals were in Medina

ALL

Panic sets in, there is nowhere to run

Gloom and doom rules, there is no solution

After this weekend the country is done

What do we do to receive absolution?

The system is crumbling, gods of finance are deaf

Bankers are traveling the road to collision

Run for the exit, call the I.M.F.

Get ammunition, dry goods, and provisions

This is the end of the civilized world

There is no light at the end of this tunnel

Money, our system's umbilical cord

went from Niagara Falls to a funnel

Gloom and doom, Gloom and doom are the words of the day

There is no hiding, all that's left is to pray

There is one message we want to convey:

This situation is here to stay!

Scene 7 - MBAs at the bar

MBA #1

I graduated at the top of my class

Not bad for a small-town kid

I was on the fast track to become top brass

I was the best of the breed

I traveled to China, Mumbai, Singapore

I flew a million miles a year

Champaign, valium and sleeping pills

Were staples for keeping in gear

I gained 40 pounds, I ate really well

I drank scotch to calm down

But after a while it all was hell

This whole ordeal made me frown

I had no home, I had no friends

There was no one I could trust

My career was on track, but my life was a dead end

I looked at it all with disgust

If I had to travel another mile

To close yet another deal

If I had to look at another file..

I felt like a hamster on a running wheel

I saw my family once a year

I know they missed me a lot

One day, though, it became very clear

That I should cut this Gordian knot

I remembered my childhood ambitions

I remembered the tavern, my friends

And then I had this premonition

That my life was about to end

And I had to ask myself what really matters

Do I want to spend my whole life on airplanes

So far away from a family warmth and chatter

Living life in the so called "fast lane"

The richest man in the cemetery

Like the poorest man are still dead

And the size of their toys does not matter

What matters is the life that they led

Their families and their friends are what matters

Their picnics and games and their kids

Their holiday dishes that clatter

And what's cooking under the lid

One day you look in the mirror

You look yourself straight in the eyes

There you'll see someone who's very dear

Congratulations! You have won the Grand Prize!

MBA #2

I worked for a major enterprise

I was happy as a clam when I was hired

But after only a short while I realized

To advance in this job was required

To arrive in the office before seven

To pretend there was much work to be done

To pretend that at work I'm in heaven

And to stay long after others have gone

The relationships were all, but artificial

And backstabbers always did their best to do their deed

I was told by a company official

That I had to bed him to succeed.

This is not what I thought I'd be doing

I was not prepared at all

Various ideas started brewing

In my mind, and then I hit the wall

Soul searching, therapy, depression

All of these ended up in vain

But, then, I remembered an old obsession

I picked up Hugo, Steinbeck, and Mark Twain

Their words, an elixir of wisdom

Woke up my desires, hopes, and mind

And the world started changing around me

I went in next morning and resigned

I resigned to go back to teaching

This is my desire and my goal

That souls of kids I will be reaching

From this point this will be my role

To the kids whose minds are still like sponges

That absorb all the knowledge and wit

I will bring Jane Austen and Jack London

To the teacher's guild I will commit

Where my real treasure will be children learning;

Knowledge is wealth that'll set them free

For true things in life they will be yearning

Building their futures is Job Number One,

Don't you agree?

MBA #3

Everything was going so well

I came I saw I conquered

Everyone else I could outsell

I've been waiting for a promotional transfer

But everything changes-

A memo came in saying our company is under investigation

I have been summoned

And I have been told

There will be a major litigation

Our top management, we were told

Defrauded a bunch of investors

Our stock disappeared, and heads rolled

This couldn't unwind any faster

That same afternoon I picked up all my stuff,

But had nowhere to go

Jobs were scarce and I've had enough

Of this crap, I felt so low...

And then the phone rang

My uncle has calling

To offer a baker's job

I jumped for joy

Picked up my coat

My body seemed to throb

And in the morning, before dawn

I started baking bread

My melancholy all, but gone

I'd never go back

There is some magic when you bake

When kids come in and cheer

But when they try your carrot cake

They think you are a hero

And you create, and mix and knead

And use imported cheese

And with each slice your soul is freed

With yourself you're at peace

There's something comforting, I'll say

When people smell fresh bread

To cheese and buttermilk – hooray!

Hooray to the freshest bread!

ALL 3

Do what you like, like what you do

Everything else is a crock

Follow your dreams, but have fun too

Anything else is just for schmucks!

Scene 8 – Financial Network

Older Man - Financial News Co-Anchor

The markets have lost half of their value

It looks very much like the worst is behind

In any event, I'd like to inform you

This whole situation was very unkind

We lost credibility

We lost bucks and hopes

And most are lucky to have any job

The country is still on a slippery slope

When I think of our nation I sob

Younger Man - Financial News Co-Anchor

Our panel of experts

Younger Woman - Financial News Co-Anchor

Oh, please I can't hear it

Younger Man - Financial News Co-Anchor (Excited)

They think that the government

Is doing its best

They want to rename our country Zimbabwe

Instead of Congress they want IRS

The mood is upbeat

China is buying paper

Looks like we avoided

A fall off the cliff

A few trillion dollars

Went up into vapor

Retirement plans

Disappeared in poof

Younger Woman - Financial News Co-Anchor

Instead of the dollar they want Russian rubles

GM will produce Chevy Vega again

We'll start making payments to Germans in strudels

And will implement a five year plan

ALL OF THEM

Hang on everybody, the crisis is ending

Forget we are broke, debt-laden, and poor

Forget that the banks have all but stopped lending

Just watch our show – it's excitement galore!

Scene 9 – Bankers at a Resort

All Bankers

We got life support from the taxpayers

We already have a second wind

We make no loans, but who cares?

We make sure that every client will be skinned

When you come to our friendly branches

Every time you pay a lot of fees

We made out good from selling swaps and "tranches"

We are coming out of the freeze

Every quarter we rack up more profits

Money is not a problem, not at all

We receive our funds, well, for nothing

There is no reason to think small

We receive our bonuses in millions

Well, one has to be sure that ends will meet

But the fact that our country's debt is in trillions

Won't affect our own balance sheet

We are getting bigger our powers are vast

We have our stock options and boats

The fact that we kind of created this mess

Is unimportant..

Politician

 Just vote!

Scene 10 - New Class of MBAs – Karl Marx and Adam Smith Present

Adam Smith

The more things change

Karl Marx

The more they stay the same

Adam Smith

A greater fool will roam the Earth forever

Human kind has no one to blame

Except themselves

For bug of greed strikes dumb and clever

Whether it's greed for gold or greed for slaves

Religious greed or greed for neighbor's wife

It only shows our society's decay

No, greed is no good; you have been fed a lie.

Karl Marx

I have to say that my capitalist friend is right

This is society's great downfall and degradation

Apparently, this is the way for a great nation

To learn the moral hazard plight

Das Kapital has flaws I admit

But what had happened here is a shame

You built a pedestal for greed

You have only yourselves to blame

Both

The more things change

The more they stay the same

Professor

What do we do?

Where do we go from here?

Don't chase a dollar

Chase your dream

Do what you like without fear

Derive your pleasure from within

We are right now at a crossroad

Where to do nothing is also a choice

Just get ready to carry your load

Nothing will change, until you raise your voice

CHORUS

Raise your voice against corruption

Raise your voice against inaction

Raise your voice for better education

Raise your voice for longer vacations

Raise your voice for accessible medical care

Raise your voice for infrastructure repair

Raise your voice for true equality

Raise your voice for life quality

Raise your voice for a modern energy grid

Raise your voice against GREED

Raise your voice against government waste

If politicians waste, then they should be replaced

Raise your voice against special-interest groups

Raise your voice to bring back our troops

Raise your voice against all kinds of crime

Raise your voice against wasting time

Raise your voice against fast food and drugs

Raise your voice against neighborhood thugs

Raise your voice for new job creation

Raise your voice to build a great nation

Raise your voice, my young friends, raise your voice

Remember: we are privileged to have a choice!

978-1-105-44387-9